HORSES IN HISTORY

By Barbara M. Linde

Gareth Stevens
Publishing

Please visit our Web site, www.garethstevens.com. For a free color catalog of all our high-quality books, call toll free 1-800-542-2595 or fax 1-877-542-2596.

Library of Congress Cataloging-in-Publication Data

Linde, Barbara M.
 Horses in history / Barbara M. Linde.
    p. cm. – (Horsing around)
Includes index.
ISBN 978-1-4339-4628-8 (pbk.)
ISBN 978-1-4339-4629-5 (6-pack)
ISBN 978-1-4339-4627-1 (library binding)
1. Horses–History–Juvenile literature. I. Title.
SF283.L55 2011
636.109–dc22

                                        2010030119

First Edition

Published in 2011 by
Gareth Stevens Publishing
111 East 14th Street, Suite 349
New York, NY 10003

Copyright © 2011 Gareth Stevens Publishing

Designer: Michael J. Flynn
Editor: Therese Shea

Photo credits: Cover, p. 1 General Photographic Agency/Hulton Archive/Getty Images; (cover, back cover, p. 1 wooden sign), (front cover, pp. 2–6, 8, 11–12, 14–16, 19–24 wood background), back cover (wood background), pp. 13, 14–15, 17 Shutterstock.com; pp. 4–5 De Agostini Picture Library/De Agostini/Getty Images; p. 7 Al Barry/Hulton Archive/ Getty Images; p. 9 Annie Griffiths Belt/National Geographic/Getty Images; p. 10 Wallace Kirkland/Time & Life Pictures/Getty Images; p. 18 MPI/Archive Photos/ Getty Images; pp. 20–21 Dorling Kindersley/Getty Images.

Printed in the United States of America

CPSIA compliance information: Batch #CW11GS: For further information contact Gareth Stevens, New York, New York at 1-800-542-2595.

Contents

Words in the glos

The first horses didn't look like modern horses. About 55 million years ago, forests covered much of North America. Many small **mammals** lived in these forests, including the first horses. Scientists call this horse *Eohippus* (ee-oh-HIH-puhs). That means "**dawn** horse."

Eohippus was small. It had a long tail and a pointy snout, or nose, like a dog. Its short teeth were good for eating leaves. *Eohippus*'s coat was probably dark with lighter spots to help it hide in forests.

Each of *Eohippus's* front feet had four toes, while each back foot had three toes.

THE MANE FACT

Each of *Eohippus's* toes was covered by a hoof.

Eohippus changed over the next few million years. By about 35 million years ago, it had longer legs that helped it run faster. Its back was longer, too. Instead of four toes on each front foot, it had three toes. It had larger teeth for eating different kinds of plants.

This horse's head was bigger. Its eyes were toward the back of its head. It could see its surroundings more easily. This animal is called *Mesohippus* (meh-zuh-HIH-puhs), which means "middle horse."

This photo shows a modern horse's skull (top) compared to the small skull of *Eohippus* (bottom).

THE MANE FACT

Scientists think the spots on horses' coats disappeared during the time of *Mesohippus*. This might mean the forests were disappearing, too.

Mesohippus **adapted** to changes in the land. Its teeth and neck got longer and stronger. It could eat tough grasses. Its eyes moved further back on its head. Now the animal could see almost all the way around itself.

By about 5 million years ago, the horse was about 50 inches (127 cm) high. Its teeth had gotten longer, too. There was just one toe on each foot. This animal was called *Pliohippus* (ply-uh-HIH-puhs), which means "more horse."

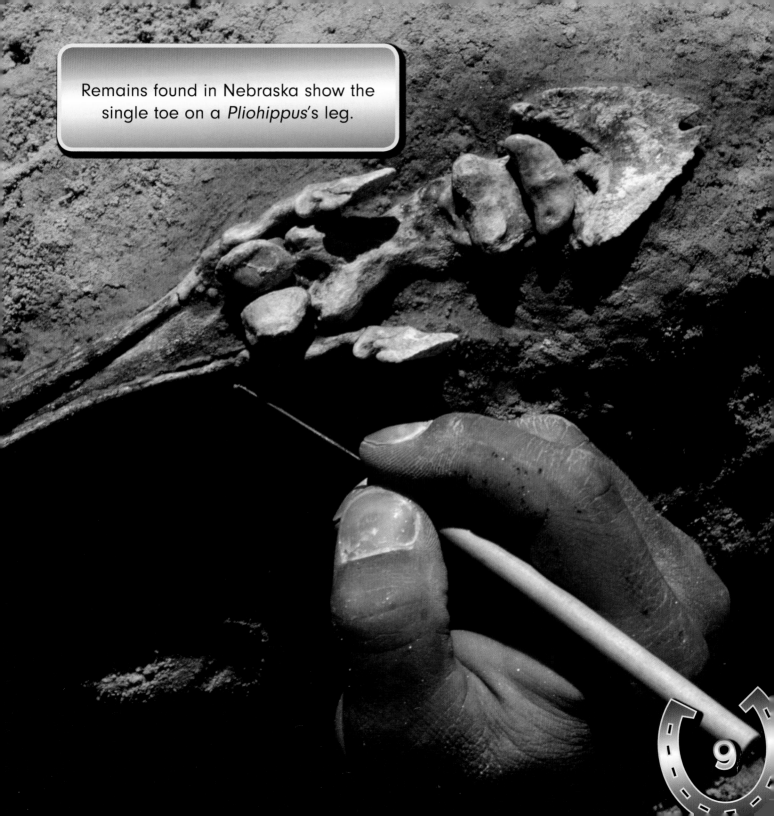

Remains found in Nebraska show the single toe on a *Pliohippus*'s leg.

This small Tarpan horse comes from the same family as a kind of early *Equus*.

The "True Horse"

Over the next few million years, *Pliohippus* changed until it looked like a small modern horse. We call this animal *Equus* (EH-kwuhs), or "true horse."

Scientists think that most **species** of *Equus* started in North America. About 3 million years ago, some species traveled to other **continents** using land bridges. After many years, water covered the land bridges. The horses in North and South America died out. Only the horses in Europe and Asia **survived**.

11

Over time, three main groups of horses survived. These groups **evolved** into modern horses. The forest horse lived in northern Europe. The Tarpan and the Asian wild horse, both in Europe and Asia, were smaller than forest horses. The Asian wild horse still exists today.

Today, horses can be divided into light horses and heavy horses. Light horses come from the Tarpan and Asian wild horse families. Heavy horses come from the forest horse family.

THE MANE FACT

Donkeys and zebras are members of the horse family.

Asian wild horses, shown here, are also called Mongolian wild horses and Przewalski's horses (named after Russian explorer N. M. Przewalski).

13

These draft horses are called Shire horses. Their thick bodies are good for pulling.

Light Horses, Heavy Horses

A light horse usually weighs less than 1,500 pounds (680 kg), and a heavy horse weighs over 1,500 pounds.

Light horses have long legs and narrow bodies. They're mostly used for riding or pulling small **carriages** or wagons. Racing horses and show jumpers come from this group.

Heavy horses are also called draft horses. They're tall with large muscles and very strong, thick legs. These animals pull heavy wagons and plow fields.

THE MANE FACT

Horses' coats are usually gray, brown, black, white, or tan. Some horses have spotted coats.

Some scientists think that people first began using horses around 4000 B.C. in the grasslands of southern Russia and central Asia. People learned how to **tame** the wild horses. They probably first used horses for food and milk. Then they learned to ride them. Finally, people figured out how to join horses to wagons and carts.

Once people began using horses for **transportation**, they could travel far from home. By 1500 B.C., people in the **Middle East** and Egypt had horses, too.

Horses were used in battle, as shown in this ancient Greek sculpture.

17

This painting of a Sioux war chief dates from 1901.

THE MANE FACT

Scientists have found drawings of horses in caves dating back to 18,000 B.C.

Horses became important in the lives of people all over Europe and Asia. Christopher Columbus brought horses to the Americas in 1493. This was the first time in thousands of years that horses had been on the American continent. Native Americans in North America learned to raise and ride horses.

In 1788, an English captain named Arthur Phillip took the first horses to Australia. They did well in their new home. The horses helped English settlers travel, plant crops, and explore the continent.

From the 1700s until about the middle of the 1900s, horses pulled plows on farms and worked in mines. Cowboys on **ranches** rode horses to move cattle. In cities, horses pulled wagons full of milk, lumber, and other supplies. They were also used for public transportation.

Mesohippus
(35 million years ago)

Eohippus
(55 million years ago)

Machines took over most hard jobs by the middle of the 1900s. Since then, horses have been used mostly for fun and sport. Wherever you go, you'll find horses—and people who love them!

Horses have evolved to become one of the most useful and beloved animals.

Equus
(3 million years ago)

Pliohippus
(5 million years ago)

Glossary

adapt: to change in order to better fit surroundings

carriage: a wheeled cart drawn by horses

continent: one of the seven large bodies of land on Earth

dawn: the beginning of something, such as a period of time

evolve: to grow and change from an earlier form

mammal: an animal with a backbone and hair that breathes air and drinks milk as a baby

Middle East: the countries of southwest Asia and northern Africa, including countries from Libya on the west to Afghanistan on the east

ranch: a farm where livestock are raised on open land

species: a group of animals that are all of the same kind

survive: to stay alive

tame: to change from a wild condition and make useful

transportation: carrying goods and people from place to place

For More Information

Books:

Clutton-Brock, Juliet. *Horse.* New York, NY: Dorling Kindersley, 2008.

Halls, Kelly Milner. *Wild Horses: Galloping Through Time.* Plain City, OH: Darby Creek Publishing, 2008.

Hendry, Linda. *Horse Crafts.* Toronto, ON, Canada: Kids Can Press, 2006.

Web Sites:

Horses
www.historyforkids.org/learn/environment/horses.htm
Read about the importance of horses throughout history, and see photos of horses in ancient times.

Horses
www.pbs.org/wnet/nature/episodes/horse/introduction/3153/
Learn about the evolution of horses and their uses today.

Index